PHYLLIS &
DOROTH   ER
PAINSWICK, GLOS'.

Telephone: Painswick 130.

HAND - PRINTED STUFFS

or dresses, fitted upholstery, curtains and covers made to order.
Made coats, bedspreads, shawls, scarves. Parcels can be sent on approval.
Visitors to the Cotswolds are invited to see the work in progress and the
finished stuffs, at Painswick. Above is a pattern of our indigo-dyeing.

Spine

Spine

Jane Weir

Templar Poetry

Published in 2012 by Templar Poetry
Templar Poetry is an imprint of Delamide & Bell

Fenelon House
Kingsbridge Terrace
58 Dale Road, Matlock, Derbyshire
DE4 3NB

www.templarpoetry.co.uk

ISBN 978-1-906285-11-1

Typeset by Pliny
Graphics by Paloma Violet

Printed in India

Author's Note

This book is not a narrative biography and like much of Barron and Larcher's work is innovative and experimental. The poems and textiles which appear tell their stories, they do not merely illustrate.

Acknowledgements

I wish to thank everyone who has helped in the course of researching and writing this book. Many thanks to Jean Vacher, Collections Manager at the Crafts Study Centre, Farnham, Surrey. Thanks are also due to Dr. Miles Lambert at The Gallery of Costume at Platt Hall and to the staff at Manchester City Art Gallery for locating two of Dorothy Larcher's watercolours.

Foreword

Their auto/biography on cloth not paper...

While I was writing *Walking The Block* I came to realise that a sequel was inevitable, *Spine* wades deeper, sinks further into the lives, work and practices; the stories of the development of the makers, dyers and handblock printers, Phyllis Barron and Dorothy Larcher.

Spine encounters borders, both real and imaginary; circling and cross-hatching their separate war experiences. Phyllis Barron served as a VAD during the First World War and her future partner, Dorothy Larcher, found herself stranded in India until after the war. *Spine* asks questions about how their direct and indirect experiences germinated within the borders of their different conscious and unconscious realities, seeping through the dye colours of their printed stuffs, clambering in Dorothy's designs, or thrashing in Phyllis's.

I wanted to explore each 'vertebra' that came to support the whole body of their printed 'stuffs'; this is what they called their printed designs. I wanted to see what they were made of, so to speak, what lay between the discs, throbbed through the nerves, flexed the sinews. Phyllis had direct experience of the wounded, the mind and the body, the soul and the soulnessness of the battlefield; this stands in stark contrast to Dorothy's experience, which on the face of it, appears to be untouched, unscathed, almost 19th Century, so immersed was she in the ancient and traditional dye practices and print techniques of India.

Yet, we know she was aware of the haemorrhage of traditional Indian handicrafts and the fierce arguments that raged about the dissolution and integration of Indian Art and Crafts into modern Western art.

I wanted to explore how the two women interacted or overprinted each other when they eventually formed a partnership; how they found common ground, amidst their difference, how they found ways to converse through pattern and colour, to create a sense of unity and harmony.

I turned their pockets inside out, so to speak, excavating turn-ups, hems, folds and seams, the patch pockets of their lives. As I wrote I found that things could never be forced open. Sometimes events and circumstances got stuck or I had to vary the pace or back off. I trusted my gut instinct so a line wouldn't get broken, at other times I let a passage fall or waste away, sometimes I let it bloom or bolt.

After a time, patches became clearer, or as Blake described it 'the bounding line' would come into view with all its inflections and movements, and I could continue.

The True Method of knowledge is experiment

William Blake: All Religions are One (1788)

How do we distinguish one from another, but by the
bounding line and its infinite inflections and movements?

William Blake: The Bounding Line

Contents

Poems & Passages

Phyllis

Dorothy

Overprinting

Dorothy to Phyllis

Phyllis & Dorothy

Fathoming the Repeat

Bibliography

Contents

Textiles & Blocks
in order of appearance

Phyllis

Dyestuffs

Plants Which Dye Red, Red, Red

Birch, *Betula alba,* Fresh inner bark.
(Mordant, wash & rinse)

Dyer's Woodruff, *Asperula tinctoria,* Roots
(Mordant, wash and rinse)

Evergreen Alkanet, *Anchusa semperbirens.*
(Mordant, wash & rinse)

Lady's Bedstraw, *Gallium boreale,* Roots.
(Mordant, wash & rinse)

Marsh Pontentil, *Potentilla comarum*, Roots.
(Mordant, wash & rinse)

Gromwell, *Lithospermum arvense.*
(Mordant, wash & rinse)

Common Sorrel, *Rumex acetosa,* Roots.
(Mordant, wash & rinse)

Wild Madder, *Rubia peregrina.*
(Mordant, wash & rinse)

Zigzag

The emerging painter, designer and printer Paul Nash, friend of the handblock printers Phyllis Barron and Dorothy Larcher, spoke passionately in his youth of London and its 'quiet spots', of those places where 'nature seemed to weave a special magic. There are places, just as there are people and objects and works of art, whose relationship of parts creates a mystery, an enchantment which cannot be analysed'.

Nash explored spaces outside the normal conventions of everydayness; he spoke of the quiet nook of Kensington Gardens and its 'uncertain difference' from the rest of the park. It was a 'wild streak in a well-brought up family, a breakaway from tradition'. For Nash it was always the 'inner life' of the subject rather than its characteristic lineaments which appealed, though that life, of course, is 'inseparable, actually, from its physical features', adding, 'the secret of a place lies there for everyone to find, though not, perhaps, to understand. I shall tell of places infinitely far removed from each other in character.'

And this vision and disposition is also true of Phyllis Barron and Dorothy Larcher and their lives as artists and makers of pattern. There they stand amidst the radiating stones, the megalithic monuments, avenues and alignments, the stones of Carnac, that ancient place in Southern Brittany.

From this distance you can just make them out, Phyllis the taller, broader, Dorothy a little further on in front, clutching her hat keenly as the wind picks up. And there is 'dislocation at first', but each can see 'little mouthfuls in each other's eyes'. Each mouthful in turn identified, internalised by them both, brought back, shook out inside the printing workshop, this essence of place with its laylines, energy seeping from each stone making shapes in the form of a pattern, a pattern developed, worked out, a pattern over time christened 'Carnac', derived from these windswept avenues, dolmens and alignments. For Phyllis and Dorothy knew, they understood their friend Paul Nash, when he spoke of 'places', his 'places'; the prehistoric sites of Avebury, the sea wall at Dymchurch, the trenches of Passchendale. They understood what he meant, the two of them standing there, Phyllis the taller, broader, Dorothy a little further on in front, dropping her hand from her hat now that the wind has eased; as artists all trying not only to find the essence of the landscape and the stonescape, but the essence of the artist, for they too are trained artists. They understood how the observer projects his or her own emotion onto the landscape, finding in its shapes, lines and contours their own 'inner life' or vision, echoing, 'Out there in the sun and the rain each stone's a mimic'.

Phyllis and Dorothy's printed stuffs, or as I call them their autobiography on cloth not paper, take on the names of people they know, 'Peach' for instance christened after their friend Harry Peach, or Clifford, christened after Phyllis's hairdresser, or Delhi and Carnac, christened after a sense of place, the essence of a place; and it is something about a place, a person; a pulse as is seen in their print 'Octopus', that makes their choice of names much more than labels merely identifying a piece of cloth for sale.

Phyllis Barron and Paul Nash both trained at the Slade School of Art, both exhibited at the influential London Group, and like Nash, Phyllis Barron served in the First World War, not as a soldier; though some would say nursing is a sort of soldiering, at the Belgium front. The saying 'you can't take the tiger out of the cat', is also true to the artist, no matter what art or craft they practice. There is always the gnawing hunger to create; somehow the imaginative process remains alert and acute, even amidst horror. And it is testimony to the men, women, numerous artists, writers, craftsmen, and the work that arose out of their experiences at home and at the front, that something always remains as a remembrance and essence of times, places and experiences seen and shared.

Paul Nash landed in France on 22nd February 1917, joining the 15th Battalion on the Ypres, Salient. He spoke of marching up to the front line, discovering 'surprising sights' amongst the destruction – spring flowers blooming everywhere, green buds on the trees in a shell-destroyed wood still 'reeking with poison gas, where nightingales sang'. Nash wrote, ' It sounds absurd, but life has a greater meaning here and a new zest, and beauty is more poignant'.

He continued to see beauty in blasted woods, ruined buildings writing of 'trenches under a bloody sort of sunset, the crescent moon sailing above'. And, 'Oh, these wonderful trenches at night, at dawn, at sundown! Shall I ever loose the picture they have made in my mind'. This is not to say he wasn't aware of the infinite slaughter and madness, the day-to-day, night-to-night, relentlessness of it all; like other men and women he was not immune to 'this monstrousness' describing the front line as a 'nightmare', where nothing 'seemed real'. There is a hint of half reality, a twilight world, Nash the Romantic follower of Samuel Palmer, the poet Blake, 'opening his eyes, looking to the skies', what he called his 'visual expansions' into Blake's 'regions of the air'. Nash wrote that 'I believe that by a process of what I can only describe as inward dilation of the eyes I could increase my actual vision. I seemed to develop a power of interpretation, which disclosed strange phenomena. I persuaded myself I was seeing visions'. You may think and you'd be partially right, that Futurism, born in Italy under the inspiration of Filippo Marinetti coupled with the English branch, Vorticism, headed by the controversial painter and writer Wyndham Lewis, had all but passed Nash by. We know that Phyllis Barron, though we are unsure about Dorothy, was inspired and fired up by the ideas of the Italian Marinetti, when he visited the Englands of 1910, 1912, and 1914.

Scan the seated crowd – there she is in the audience. We know that Phyllis attended lectures at the Victoria and Albert Museum and the British Museum Libraries, consulting dye books, reading about pattern and print techniques, sinking inside centuries. Is that Phyllis in the front row? No! There she is at the back, next to the slouchy gentleman in a moleskin coat.

We know she was influenced by Vorticists, and by Wyndham Lewis, who toured and exhibited works by members of the movement. As she walked the Hampstead streets, full of the rhythms of print and surface pattern, every pigeon, every railing presented itself as a possible motif. Up close her brain whirls away like a street bicycle through Modernity, sweeping away the stultifying past, absorbing the present and the new forms it took; the motions of machines, the life and death in the trenches, the relentless barbed wire, the mud and the deafening blast and roar of the battlefields of Europe seeping into, spilling over her printed stuffs.

Vorticist art, geometric in form, intense in colour and wildly abstract was concerned with the flux of war machines, their destructive intensity, set within natural places in all their bombed-out, crushed-underfoot, blasted-to-smithereen-ness. Phyllis knew it well and at the closest quarters she dealt with it every day as a VAD, dealt with its devastating effects literally and subconsciously, knew how this impacted on her imagination under pressure, aware in the volta of pattern how her printed stuffs; their colour, their patterns in all their faux sobriety, across table tops, chair backs, behind windows in haunted dusky squares in London and upholstered window seats in rural Gloucestershire, all rolled out in their treacherous beautiful wretchedness.

Once the Vorticist zigzag was born Phyllis, always the block printer, could apply the zag its ziggy-ness, to seconds, hours, days; she had long had the zigzag inside her head, ricocheting again and again like fork lightning from side to side before she put it down on paper: an envelope? Then cut it into the face of a block, walked it across length after length of cloth. She had it, yes she did, long into the stations of each night.

Looking at her print 'Spine' you wonder, if despite her almost holy respect for craftsmanship and natural forms, whether she questioned how this hands-on craft-controls-everything-from-start-to-finish philosophy could represent what she had witnessed in all its stinking horror; Vorticism offered her consciousness and her conscience respectively a way out and a way inside all of this. We know she took things personally, chastising William Morris in a letter, though he was long dead, for abandoning natural dyes. But people change, events change them, sometimes forever, sometimes only for the moment before they change back again.

Paul Nash wrote enthusiastically, after seeing his friend the painter Christopher Nevinson's dry point etching *Ypres After The First Bombardment* (1916), 'It is part of the world I am interested in... I begin to believe in the Vorticists doctrine of destruction – almost'. Only later did he describe in a letter to his wife 'the slaughterhouse, a nightmare of a country more conceived by Poe or Dante than by nature, unspeakable, utterly indescribable. In the fifteen drawings I have made I may give you some idea of the horror...'

Phyllis the textile artist, printer and dyer, tending the bodies and minds of men and boys witnessed and dealt with the same inferno, confronted the consequences of each day, each night, herself. And as she sat quietly, dead on her feet inside her tent we can only imagine how she would survive to bear witness, as Nash did, in patterns, in prints, in essence, those fragments of feeling that remain of madness and rage, hollowness and sorrow, with the inside barely holding and the outside hammering in.

.

Passageway

Pulling off my gloves
felt as if my hands
were skinned.
Taut as a brace of rabbits
not long from the field
they had the high putty-like
gloss of devilled kidneys.
Lifting up my hat
felt as if my head
was scalped,
and no way of inspecting.

Time trickled like sand
inside an hour glass,
tipping the passage
one way then another.
Orderlies dashed
behind bubbled lantern glass
like the Paris Morgue,
as described by Dickens.

I remember slabs & sluices,
troughs gurgling & holes seeping
& rows of arms & legs,
half heads & full heads
twisted, yanked back,
& one eye & another eye half closed,
all eyes turned inward on blackness
like ice plants & mouths puckering
like bacilli spores,
iron black, dabs of russet,
mildew of sores.

Everywhere the glutted re-workings
of the dead,
hang from pegs.

To The New Girl With The Shaking Hand

I say stitches need not always match.
Tiny flaws, irregularities,
inevitable with the hands-on process.

Steel yourself. Ease the skin forward – back.
I remember my first day, mistaking iodine for indigo.

You Can Tell When A Wound Is Healing

around the edges, fronds of quercitron,
a placid, warm water yellow.

Whilst Tending Wounds, Stemming Infection

scrutiny delivers a portmanteau of thoughts.

In combination weld & iron which, when discharged,
gives a sluggish, greenish Mary Shelley yellow.

Crusts Have Formed Across The Wounds

like grey backs.

When you prod, for you have to prod sometimes,
they hisssssssssssssss, hissing at each other
like cockroaches crossing the Château's cellar floor.

The Night Before I Tipped His Head

broke the rules, answered,
Yes, it's Mother, yes son, I'm here.

A gardener he was, fond of Hollyhocks,
spiky, sulphur Mallow.
His lips upswept,
a culvert blocked with Autumn leaves.
I trickled a mixture of brandy champagne,
let his head drop when I felt him go.
I swilled, marbling the cup.

When I See A Face Wound

I say quickly to myself,
detach Phyllis, detach.

Do as Sister says, sustain a smile
even at this close-quarter-business.
Adjust face, lift the tip of his flap,
enter suffering, overprint, saying:

Remember a pattern unit need not be drawn.
Remember the night blind, its staccato print.
Remember to dumb down the razzmatazz of dazzle.
Remember don't think, Do!

Do? What shall I do with my eyes?
Drop them like dots inside apron pockets.
Blood shot dots –
will they come in useful?
Do? What shall I do with my ears?

The difficulty lies when the wounds are healed.
The surgeon did his best –
still a gargoyle.

There Goes The Horn, More Wounded Arrive

Out there, no solid sound, no tone,
no abstract to detonate, no steadfast pitter-patter,
no zigzag to race, no striding lighthouse beam to guide.

There goes the horn, the wounded stack & pile.
Men. How to describe the cot cased?
Men. Put back, lopped off, blunt as toe-caps.
Boys. Stretchered, slumped & shored.
Heaps of rag-doll men, heaps of rag-bone boys
they tremble, lull then moan.

And afterwards,
lay amid the boom & chink
I beg exhaustion,

Put me out.

To An Unnamed Zigzag On Your Difficult Birth

To the right, attended by dull yellow spikes.
To the left, attended by solemn discs.
Beneath a black sky, mignonette moon, my hand.
With this I copyright, catalogue, suppress.

Battleship Zigzag

First, his brusque embrace in *Harris Tweed*,
reminiscent of fox terrier fur & the early 1940's.
Then, his apology for scuffing my cheek, being an old man,
to top it all a southerner.

I tried to place the accent, Portsmouth, Southampton,
             Zennor?
We shared a love of Z's as do the Cornish & Venetians.
We shared a love of Zigzags & Chevrons.
We shared a love of a footballer, Zinedine Zidane.
We shared a love of Zabaglione.
We shared a love of Dazzle.

I spoke of my Father's Doctor in Vicenza, Dr Zing, a Venetian.
He spoke of his Father, his boyhood,
how together they watched the transformation of battleships
from flat, matt, grey.
Zigzags, jostling, jarring, elbowing, disrupting,
resisting the flat, matt, grey
until the flat, matt, grey
has never been.

We agreed,
grimacing through the North Atlantic chop,
         no direct hits.

"Spine"
Printed
in
Blue
on
Undyed
Organdie

"Spine"

Some things we didn't share,
like marriage to men,
though I had my moments.
Some things we did share,
like a merging of minds,
drawing down of blinds
& the steep descent into pattern.
You knew about pattern,
you said so, I read so
in your scribbled sample book,
read your curious puritan
pronouncements
on the principles of design.

Through the wallpaper
you spied figures creeping,
fronds of figures choking;
battle of a window latch & ivy.
Behind each bar of your bed,
inch by inch, tracking
where the pattern lolled
like hundreds of broken necks
& hundreds of bulbous eyes
stare yellow, blood shot
& yellow & upside down –
I identified.

On horn-less nights I found myself
as you found yourself,
dragged across the floor.
Each pair of stalking eyes on slanting stalks,
giving way to the next stage of malady.

Not for me the wall, lane, stage-lit
by moonlight, rather how to untangle
a mangle of men from the shape
of bones more bones & only bones,
backbones turned this way that,
backbones jangling, backbones
that gurned & grimaced
clunked like wind charms.

Things can't be arranged or rearranged
or played like a funny bones xylophone,
along the lines of any rational laws.
Alteration, symmetry or repetition,
what you called a *lurid debased Romanesque*.
Lazy eyed, I too grow excited tracking.

Charlotte's Jaunty Yellow

(Phyllis to Charlotte)

There are things inside the pattern no one knows but me,
or ever will.

Do you know the colour yellow?

(Charlotte to Phyllis)

Yes, the colour is repellent, almost revolting; a smouldering unclean
yellow.
Strangely faded by slow turning sunlight.

A dull lurid orange, in some places a sickly sulphur tint.
It makes me tired to follow it.

(Phyllis to Charlotte)

Yellow, I followed it once, twice, No, thrice,
like an orrery around the room it spun.

(Charlotte to Phyllis)

Yes, it's crafty; dull enough to confuse the eye in following,
pronounced enough to irritate, provoke study.
When you follow the lame uncertain curves for a little
distance they suddenly commit suicide –
plunge off at outrageous angles, destroy themselves in unheard
contradictions.

(Phyllis to Charlotte)

The front pattern does move and no wonder...

(Charlotte to Phyllis)

No wonder. No.

(Phyllis to Charlotte)

Like La Fanu's green monkey, it too turned yellow, swinging,
circling, stabbing gluts of fruited seams.

I know the pattern well – do we agree?

(Charlotte to Phyllis)

Yes.
The outside pattern is a florid arabesque, reminding one of
              fungus.
Imagine a toadstool in joints, an interminable string of
              toadstools,
budding & sprouting in endless convolutions,
         why that is something like it.

(Phyllis to Charlotte to Anyone Who's Listening...)

Like it, it is like it. Yes.

Though, there are things inside the pattern no one knows
         but me, or ever will.

Shawl, wool, hand printed with fine fawn coloured wool
with hand printed pattern of eight feathery chevron bands
in black and green radiating outward from a central yellow
star and spaces in between and each band filled with a single
radiating yellow, a black star and smaller yellow stars.
Border pattern of groups of radiating chevrons and spots
alternating with black and green spears, alternating black.

Stricken Fields

Shall I ever yield the mysteries of those stricken fields?

Or loose the land-backed patterns, battles struck across my mind.
Or beat away a ragged moon, its shape lost behind shards of treetops.

Shall I ever yield the mysteries of those stricken fields?

Or from the crush, construct a narrative,
hope the linen union will hold, hope it'll drum in time to a colour
not sink into shade, edge into fade.
And when I dream, how will I know when to stop asking,
or know when not to lean too long or wait on answers?

And what of the men? There was drizzle as they lay dying.
They must have heard the bees buzzing, birds flying.
And the creatures, as they scurried across the earth,
what did they make of the men, ways they were lying?

Shall I ever yield the mysteries of those stricken fields?

And what of the women? There was blackness, as they slept.
They must have heard the lists read, seen the toll of shells.
And the creatures, scuttling across the pantry shelves,
what did they make of the women, when they heard them crying?

Shall I ever yield the mysteries of those stricken fields?

What use is my pen drawing before the scoop of a lantern?
Lines cannot be bore down upon, looped or scooted round,
gone is love expressed in the span of curves, live nerves,

the creeping pattern & fields surge before me,
go straight down, blacken at the tip. Lines larking, radiating
sunrise yellows & greens & bitter black stars.

I never knew stars existed. Black stars, small black stars radiating,
& spots, spots radiating chevrons, radiating green spears,
& now as the orderly shuffles, how do I manage to wake,
raise my head, curled like small crescent across my chest?

Goodbye

Not the house,
not the place
to break news
such as this.

Here, take my arm.
lets wade through
a meadow that heaves
& sighs, slams stragglers,
buttercups, poppies,
against dry stone walls.

Walking won't lessen
what I have to say,
still you have the flame,
bright instinctive feeling.
I sense this in the rise
of your oil-lamp gaze,
the way your look
smoulders.

Though beneath
the dread,
beneath the splay,
your dusky
fall-away,
your hands churn,
& the faint
wheeze of your breath,
grasping hopelessness.
Surely things can't be that bad?

I did my best
dividing light
from dark,
choosing where
& when
faint hope
might shine.

Turning at the Oak
we traipsed
back to Overton.
All around the fields
were down & the hedges
crouched cut down
& the earth clotted,
charcoaled carrion.

Even now
at this final hour,
the air between us
throbbed magpie blue.
Fragments of ghost stars
permeated,
eked the moon
like iron filings.

I turned
sloped away
to the sound of sobbing,
my footsteps stamping
all semblance of light.

'Pamela' Omega Workshop, 1914

I assure you death existed.
Why filter horror through a woman's name?

'Pamela' upholsters a chair.
I witnessed the advance.
Mounting, re-mounting arm rests,
careering down back rests, infringing cabriole legs.

When I'm asked, *What was it like?*
I, unlike the pattern, never deny being there.

1914, Working With Red In A Field Hospital, Belgium

Back in the workshop I look
for any kind of flux, discrepancy,
or break from the uniform,
when dyeing wild madder with gromwell,
or common sorrel with bedstraw, but not here.

The men lie, abstract shapes & sizes
angled & shattered in beds,
a fraction between types & ages.
Without exception all dye red,
grimy sheets, make do blankets.

I notice little variation in shade
or depth of shade, or length of spread or seep,
or smear or splatter;
where the bandage unravels,
or the flesh stitches bloom & split.

Take this boy – he won't mind me showing you.
His wound replicates early nineteenth century anilines –
look closely at his right buttock,
see mauve going green, going flinch black –
no amount of handiwork can stop
the corruption that imprints flesh,
there are no mordants for miles around.

Identifying A Pattern, After Treatment

The curator's voice thin, weak watered-down bleach,
warning the cloth's much leached, rat-nibbled, tank-trod.
Merciless, he draws down acid-free tissue
& I wish my eyes three times coated with Kevlar,
wish my ears stoppered by dead mens' fingers.

The fragment shows pattern after treatment.
Part of the repeat lies in tatters, unfathomable.
Part of the repeat healed & thickened.
Some lines sacrificed
to close the throb of chevrons, staunch bleeds.
This leaves a pattern out of sync, lop-sided,
& expression gurning, a slight moon-lit asylum,
whimsical, but not unpleasant
on a night with nightingales airing.

How long can I stay focussed?
I try turning my eyes from the black-shot border.
Turning eyes is a difficult business,
like a bisque doll I swivel my head several times,
until I face its glance full on, run on with it.
I nod, I owe it this at least; though I've seen enough,
long before he sees I'd seen enough,
and finds mercy drawing the tissue back.

Paul Nash's Table

Asked what I preferred
I said, *The simple forms of Gimpson's Oak & Birch.*

Far from the meadows, hedge rows
of Gloucestershire, Modernism lurched,
reared like a war horse's head
kicked in the belly by spurs.

The spirit was right, yet the earth
tilted like a waiter's tray,
so much so the seas ran off
& the moon, the sun rose twice,
doubled back, rose twice again
high above a starless heaven.

Somehow they wouldn't do,
Simple forms of Gimpson's Oak & Birch.
Odd, as a parrot swinging
aimless on a bamboo perch.
No, it wouldn't do.
He nodded, asked, *What can be done?*

I urged, *Light, steel & glass.*
In France I saw an operating table
fit for four to sit around.

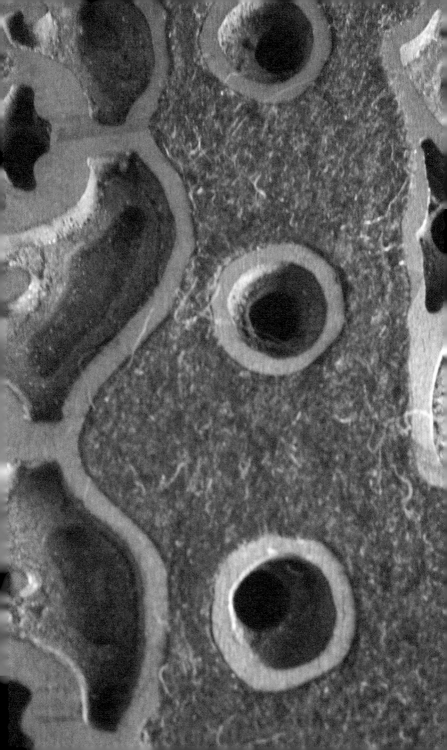

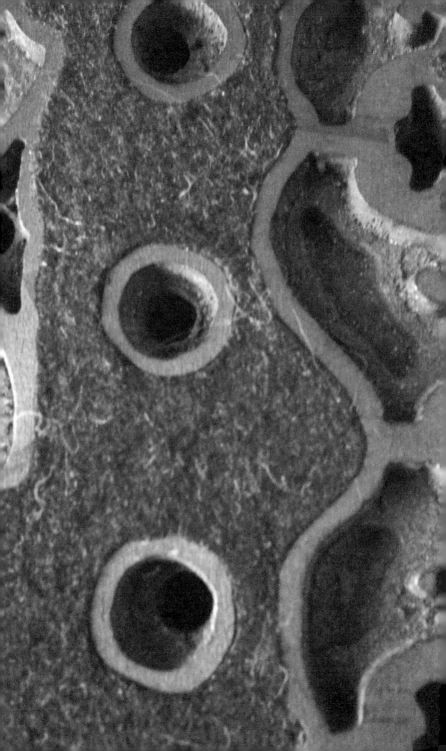

Printed Stuffs

Walking The Blocks, Blocks, Blocks

"Log"
(mallet strike)
Iron on Linen

"Scallop"
(mallet strike)
Galled Linen in Iron

"Hazlitt"
(mallet strike)
Indigo Discharge on White Cotton

"Lyon"
(mallet strike)
Indigo Discharge on Heavy Natural Linen

"Elizabethan"
(mallet strike)
White Balloon Cotton with Indigo Print

"Railway"
(mallet strike)
Positive Print Iron on Linen

"Carnac"
(mallet strike)
Indigo Discharge on White Cotton

"Dent"
(mallet strike)
Printed in Red on Heavy Undyed Linen

"Spine"
(*mallet strike*)
 Printed in Blue on Undyed Organdie

"Carnac"
(*mallet strike*)
Indigo Discharge on White Cotton

Swatch

I stand in front of the kitchen window. I'm holding a butternut squash.
If I could I'd stand outside in the yard, look in on myself, take stock,
standing, comically obscene, like a stone age fertility goddess.
From the window looking outward into the yard, turning my thoughts
inward, thinking this squash needs heavy-duty peeling,
imagining how the word *Oslo* like an *Ogee* would make a print.
Thinking through Phyllis & Dorothy & a whole day of writing.

Today I thought myself into Phyllis,
Phyllis before the war, Phyllis standing in stout brogues
sinking into the forest floor, staring at piles of birch logs,
silver, stacked inside the cleft of a Jekyll wheelbarrow.
How when she returned, thinking what it was like,
knowing the men who sawed, knowing the men who stacked
the logs are scattered far & wide,
in high summer risen, sprung through red.

Is that what she thought when she returned to Blighty?
Is that what she thought when she took up "Log",
again, & printed furiously; stamping *so much for The Green Man?*
So much for the men, who felled the birch? Gone.
And the woods gone, silent except for one, two, three, four,
woodpigeons on the splintered floor.

I stand in front of the kitchen window. I'm holding a butternut squash.
My reflection mocks. I hate being in.
It's not the same as standing outside looking in,
or up toward the Grange, as Heathcliff looked
toward the Grange, bashing his head, over & over,
how it bled all over, & now it's raining,
& is that my outline quivering?

Dorothy

Dyestuffs

Plants Which Dye Blue, Blue, Blue

Devil's Bit, *Scabiosa succisa*, Leaves prepared like Woad.
(Mordant, wash & rinse)

Dog's Mercury, *Mercurialis perennis.*
(Mordant, wash & rinse)

Privet, *Ligustrum vulgare*, Berries.
(Mordant, wash & rinse)

Red bearberry, *Arctostaphylos uva-ursi.*
(Mordant, wash & rinse)

Sloe, *Prunus communis*, Fruit.
(Mordant, wash & rinse)

Whortleberry or Blaeberry, *Vaccinium myrtillus*, Berries
(Mordant, wash & rinse)

Woad, *Isatis tinctoria*
(Mordant, wash & rinse)

Japanese Indigo,
(Mordant, wash & rinse)

Root Of The Yellow Iris,
(Mordant, wash & rinse)

Yellow Iris, *Iris pseudocoius,* Roots.
(Mordant, wash & rinse)

Elder, *Sambucus nigra,* Berries.
(Mordant, wash & rinse)

East India Company Stamped On Her Sleeves

So what do we know of Dorothy Larcher? We can pinpoint the permanency, things solid and fixed, we can pin them like badges to her chest, the date and place of her birth, the date and place of her death, in India the sail boats listing across her Indigo headscarf, and we can trace back through the family attic of stuff, the Mother, Father, she was of a modest income and not as well-off as Phyllis. We know she was artistically gifted and as a student attended the Hornsey School of Art, as a teacher taught for a while, first in England, then India, Calcutta we think, and the latter born out of an invitation from the aristocrat Christiana Lady Herringham; Dorothy had a passion for the art and crafts of India. And we know that Dorothy in India, as companion and assistant to Christiana, traced, mapped and charted the Buddhist Frescoes of The Ajanta Caves. It sounds like the origins of a myth; a Dulac fairy tale.

Half close your eyes and you can see; look there they are hard against the page, Christiana, Dorothy, fine illustrations, swaying inside the pages of a calf bound, gold stamped, perhaps a Blackie's volume. And there is Christiana, holding the rough, locally made steps, and up there Dorothy, wearing a headscarf, perched on the highest rung, swaying precariously, pale light dipping, cuckooing amidst the cave's chill. We know that Christiana went back to England leaving Dorothy behind in Calcutta with an Indian Family, trading English for Indigo and the handicrafts she admired and the print and dye techniques of a continent; returning to England in nineteen twenty three, though some say a little earlier, some say a little later.

We know what others have said of Dorothy, and for a while let me show you a fraction of what they saw; I'll thread you through their eyes. Forever, or so it seems, Dorothy's to be placed in 'contrast' to Phyllis, bold black lines between them. Reading Robin Tanner's, the painter, etcher and close friend who created the archive of Phyllis Barron and Dorothy Larcher, descriptions of them at home in Hambutts house in Gloucestershire is like stumbling upon a long lost love letter; so smitten, so absorbed is he by the two of them set in their surroundings. In the transcript of a talk he gave in the 1970's, at The Holburne Museum and Crafts Study Centre, Bath, the title does not contain Dorothy's name; it simply states Phyllis Barron 1890-1964. This is curious; yet Dorothy is present, is vital.

Dorothy looms large, equal to Phyllis, yet described as 'small, of equally strong personality' having a 'rather sad, quiet voice and a serious manner'; here again is the Phyllis to Dorothy contrast, 'her sense of humour was every bit as keen as Barron's' and Dorothy was 'beautifully dressed'. We know that she not only dressed beautifully but was, 'a most distinguished embroideress. I observed at once the immaculate stitchery and the embroidered collar and cuffs of her dress, and the amber glass buttons chosen with perfect appropriateness'. Robin places himself inside the room, yet you feel he is some distance away, '(Coffee was) served in fragile old French Cups, and we sat talking and laughing… in a room that seemed to me more harmoniously and subtly beautiful than any I had seen. Curtains, covers, cushions, were all their own, and each was printed in a scale exactly for its purpose and with a character exactly right for its purpose and with a character exactly appropriate to the setting. Every small detail of every object in the room seemed right.. I thought if ever there was a marriage of true minds it was here in this room.'

He concludes that Dorothy's 'attitude to life was more deeply hidden behind a veil of reserve and retiring nature.'

So it comes as something of a shock hearing Enid Marx, one of Britain's first multi-disciplinary designers and first apprentice of Phyllis and Dorothy, comes as a shock, hearing Enid speak of Dorothy's competitiveness when she saw one of Enid's own newly printed designs, the quiet, reserved Dorothy says, 'Damn it all, I was going to do that!'

Here is Dorothy, no, not at all small, not at all the 'small, quiet person.. hidden behind a veil of reserve..' This is another Dorothy entirely: if only we had more of this, 'Damn it all, I was going to do that!'

It was Enid Marx, known to her friends as 'Marco', who borrowed Poiret's phrase, 'It was in the air' and emphasised the dissemination of her diverse influences, including West African art, Diaghilev's Ballet , radical periodicals, including *Queerschunit*, not all consciously absorbed. Enid recalls, 'It was very interesting how these ideas do float, like the wind blowing seed from a tree'. For Enid, Dorothy and Phyllis, the use and experimental application of a Banksia Seed to cloth seems perfectly apt, in harmony with their expressed beliefs in terms of eclecticism and modern design. This brings us to indigo and Dorothy's time espent in India which echoes the idea of ideas floating around, 'in the air', on the page, changing like indigo on air, air on indigo, the incantations of indigo and what to do as it metamorphoses,

give the hands-
as well as the head
something fitting to do,

while you watch
the cotton billow,
come greenish blue,
allow 60 seconds-
blue,
come blue, bluer

Blue.

The shamenistic properties of indigo, the dye both Phyllis
and Dorothy were obsessed with, raises its head again in
the shape and perhaps the shades and tones of a headscarf.
We have a photograph of Dorothy wearing a headscarf, an
indigo headscarf, for this is India where Indigo has a shrine.
Enid Marx talks of how as a girl she cut her first stencils and
printed a scarf, yet we have no knowledge how Dorothy's
headscarf came to be; all we have is India and a ghostly
photograph, so we speculate. We are told that Dorothy sits
as part of the Ajanta group, in the November of 1910 or
1911, third row, third from the left, and she is wearing a
headscarf. Was it dyed in India? Was it dyed in indigo? Was it
block printed by herself? Dorothy's face is turned from the
side, like a lot of her individual designs which also turn away,
are fathomless, placed next to Phyllis's zigzags, chevrons.
Occasionally there is a glimpse of fuzz, bleed, some pinking
around the edges and overlaps, and it's plain to see her love of
swagger, especially in her printed designs, and particularly in
one of her most popular, "Basket".

The demand for "Basket" proved great, and commercially so.

Dorothy was on the cusp of the age departing. In household furnishing and dress prints the public appetite for flowers remained constant; more flowers, only flowers,blossoms and twigs. The vocabulary of the garden was insatiable and reminds us these are images plucked from an urbane life, whereas at times, looking at many of Phyllis's designs we are reminded of strain and tension, so fractured, so violent is the blast and jab.

With Dorothy's printed stuffs we have no memories of trauma, conflict and the sepsis, the sub-consciousness of war. Out of the partnership Phyllis appears the most modern, the most contemporary, and the most fully formed in terms of the *zeitgeist* branded upon her memory and experience..

The contrast is very striking, their experiences of wartime continents apart. We know that Dorothy went to India with Christiana Lady Herringham, we know she was marooned and could not, perhaps did not want to take a passage back to England, and we know she stayed on in Calcutta, living with an Indian family, learning the techniques and processes of traditional Indian print and dye techniques. We know she felt passionately and was, like so many others at the time, excited by the applied arts of the Indian subcontinent.

In 1878 William Morris and Edward Burne-Jones, John Everett Millais and Walter Crane petitioned the British Government for the preservation of India's indigenous craft industries. Like many Morris regarded India as the 'cradle of the industrial arts' and as a vital source of education and inspiration for British designers. Morris added that 'Englishmen in India are, in their shortsightedness, actively destroying the very sources of that education – jewellery, metalwork, pottery, calico- printing brocade weaving and carpet making'. However the early modern response went beyond handicrafts, concerning itself with painting and sculpture as well. Sir George Birdwood, the art referee for the Indian Section at South Kensington Museum, although a keen Arts and Crafts disciple, was reluctant to recognise India's fine art, such as wall paintings and sculptures. In a second wave of interest Roger Fry recognised Indian wall paintings and sculptures as 'a vast mass of new aesthetic experience', the equal to Western art.

Dorothy's response, along with many other inter-war artist craftsmen and women, was to the philosophies of Indian craft. It was the practices and techniques involved in the making, the integrity of the crafts and craftsmanship that mattered. There is a carbon tracing of Dorothy Larcher's work, published by the India Society in 1915, taken directly from the Ajanta Caves which shows two women in a palace garden. There are animals, a small temple lion not dissimilar to the winged lions of Venice, a variety of birds and a fragile deer of some sort, perhaps an onyx, kissing the slender fingers of women. And there are bunches of fruit and lush flowers suspended like lanterns that make up the backdrop, and it's the fruited-flowers, exuberant clusters, with their affinity to the printed pattern motifs to come which are reflected in the heart and soul of Dorothy's stuffs.

So what are we to make of Dorothy's designs? Sometimes we glimpse Dorothy and Christiana riding the back of a bullock cart, trundling to the caves through a rutted river bed, camped out in tents, cursing the lamps in the darkness and damp, flicking bats from their faces as they stoop to get up close to a deity or Buddha. Sometimes we feel the war never happened. It's as if Christiana and Dorothy were locked inside an air-pocket; there is a sense that the Empire still burns as bright as a tiger stripe in the night, yet the reality and consequences of the First World War. It appears simply that modernity had not dawned upon them both as one supported the other, when the lamps did not light and sheets of tracing paper, as large as eight feet by ten cocooned them. And intuitively a companionship over time evolved, as one jumps clear from a ladder, whilst the other keeps balance, keeps hold. Some say Christiana was the model for Mrs Moore in E.M. Forsters *Passage To India*, but what of Dorothy? Did Forster know of Dorothy, the one that held the ladder, who alternately lit the lamps, Dorothy the indigo addict and hand block printer? Dorothy whose face also gazed into the moonlit waters of the Ganges.

Dorothy's later partnership with Phyllis Barron was enriched by her knowledge of block-printed Indian textiles and embroideries; we see it in her designs, follow the intricate patterns' trail and colour palette. Perhaps it was the ancient tradition and longevity of Indian inspired designs that informed her work, and that merged so well with Phyllis's designs, aesthetically and philosophically and gave continuity and spiritual integrity to her own individual designs. Dorothy's patterns seem to be whole, a body intact, the rhythms steady and controlled, her vocabulary doesn't thrash or ask for anything, rather it offers something, something that you long for, a version of English certainty, a truism, and at times an imperial eccentricity. We see this eccentricity and detail again in her watercolour paintings, such as *Black and White Pansies* and *White Centaureas*.

Black and White Pansies, a still life group of black and white pansies and droopy broad ribbed leaves is all set off in a footed glass on a tabletop with something both of Constance Spry, the flower arranger and interior designer and Eric Ravilious and Edward Bawden would recognise the lacy mat, upon which the vase sits, serrated at its edges, the pale net curtains providing a back drop, a single fallen petal lounging to the left of the vase foot. Although the composition may be traditional, there is nothing of the Bournemouth here in terms of the familiar striped deck chair and beach hut; it's too spiky at the edges, too grainy and flecked, yet it would sit without anyone noticing in a vicarage or dower house. Again, we see this in "*Delhi*", the colours of an Indian summer, the cinnamon and mace, "*Delhi*", its birth certificate says, *printed in iron and synthetic red on buff, on handwoven cotton.*

Of "*Delhi*" the print only a fragment piece remains. It could be an embroidery, the delicacy of its weave, snake-like structure, its flower heads more akin to star anise, exotic, but not too exotic, sort of in-and-out of England and India, like looking inside a fruit wood box in an English kitchen, lightly spiced, aromatic, traditional. This is one of the ways of thinking through Dorothy, but it is only the beginning, for somewhere overseas Marco Polo sneezed, a tiger roared, somewhere on the quayside her sleeves got stamped…

Handicrafts

Who'll staunch the bleed
from a thousand years of handicrafts?
Took less than ten to adulterate.
Yet I believe! Try to retrieve.
I watch the procession pass.
Hand beaten jewellery, metalwork,
pottery, calico printing,
brocade weaving, carpet making,
tie-dye, ikat, block printing,
merchants bound for the sickly
gas light greens of Europe,
where streams of synthetic dyes overflow,
insinuating crude fugitive tendencies.
Who'll staunch the bleed?
I believe! Try to retrieve.

Natural Dyes

All dyes are not eternal,
the sun lightening, beautifying,
consuming;
yet look upon a Gothic room,
hung with fading tapestries.
See how colours in fade
remain ravishing,
never, even after long wearing
loose full bloom
or pass into nothingness,
or go through stages
of livid ugliness,
distinguishing the brash
of commercial from fade.
As a rose fades,
bright greens turn sheer drab,
& fashionable blues emulate indigo,
turn salty purple by candlelight,
& Prussian blues are much damaged.
Commercial Green, known as Gaslight Green,
as abominable by daylight as by gaslight,
& most agree, make the unlit midnight hideous.

Liberty

Oh! If I had one wish I'd wish
I was a Mogul Prince
and fly my hunting hawk,
shaking off anklets, bell-less jesses,
watch the hawk pick off dumpy
flightless names evocative of Liberty's East,
pluck the feathered breasts of
Poonah Thistle, Allahabad, Marigold,
Chambra Chrysanthemum, Rangoon Poppy.

"Delhi"

War broke,
nailed, *You'll live,*
full square to my forehead.
I did the dreary clubhouse rounds
of *Well Miss, tut-tut, well I don't know,*
when I spoke of staying,
trading English for Indigo.
It wouldn't have mattered,
if like a Sickert model
I'd changed my mind;
too late, India was my date.
On the quayside
a lithe temple monkey guide
stood invisible by my side,
as hat-less, waving I cut myself away.
Dorothy, marooned, castaway,
some might say stowaway.
Not for me the clearing station,
iodine, greybacks, raggle-taggle lines.
At night I slept, holding firm
to the tail-end of my dream,
trudging behind a lumbering
bullock cart back & back again
to the astonished caves,
lugging confusion about the place
as Forster lugged confusion about the place,
reading between the politeness of lines,
reading between the canter & taper of space,
Cobra's face, waiting on the echoes,
whenever, in whatever voice they came
& went & came again.

Indigo Eye

Everywhere there are parrots,
snowdrop whites
on hopping scarlet feet
& twittering malformed monkeys
too numerous to describe,
except they're tiny,
& there are black lions
with no other visible colour or mark,
& there are peacocks
of another stately sort than ours,
triangular, handsomer,
& hens too, unlike ours,
& they grow a spice, *Quilon brazil*,
& pepper in abundance,
speckling fields & woods,
gathered through May, June, July.
The village indigo has the eye,
all knowing indigo left rootless,
left to rot in water tubs,
left beneath the blazing sun to bake,
coagulating to paste,
before being rolled & chopped
into centipede segments.
& like the peacock fanning blue-eyed-green,
& like the wolf batting blue-eyed-green,
all the better to see you with.

In India, Accompanying Lady Herringham At The Ajanta Caves

Inside the caves she contemplates the frescoes, *Miracle of Sarati*,
whilst I take notes, listen to her voice tap out verbatim;
& it's incredible, I know, yet this contrast between us works.
Although she has rigour, purpose, & I the verve to carry on
in heat, it seems she can't get beyond the vitality of surface,
of the chaityas & viharas, of legends & divinities,
of the staccato sound of indigenous words spoken.

Now she is telling me she would like to come at night,
enter its mouth when the last skid of orange disappears,
& the fast flowing river burns at its edges like the ear
of someone being talked about, & she's telling me how
armed with net, a candle lit & lifted, she might see if streaked
gold goes red, is affected by the dizzying flight path of bats.

She is surface, all surface, cannot see, what lies beyond
the fragmentary, & erosion is technique, the teachings of a life;
such as how the chisel struck, first the features of the rock –
made rough enough, to hold the plaster, & as with the coming
of the rains, how plaster came into being, made from clay,

& by a skilled hand, how the finite drawings were done,
in a flash, colours applied, with plaster wet, so that in time
each colour succumbs to the figures like desire,
& as with a true love threatened, won't peel or decay,
holds true, & fades, fades, fades ever so…

chaityas are sanctuaries , viharas are monasteries

Home

In the cave
I sink to my knees,
pan out like a snow melt.
Sometimes lamps don't light,
tricky combination of air & oil,
always anxiety, coaxing compression.
Judge the mantles or they'll judge themselves.

I see sacred, spots, dots, dabs,
magic fruits, flowering trees low to the ground,
two women crouching by a pool as a tiger prowls
around a tamarind tree. Buddha's go untraced.

Above cave bats strike up like flint naps,
a helter skelter of swelter, swooping, striking
through the gloom, gibbering in sooty lairs.
Christiana cries, *You might stand a chance of catching one -
there - high, along the pleated run.*
No turning back.
I clamber the ladder, snatch, snap
like a chicken bone.

"Basket"

One of the first blocks I ever cut
& still as popular.
I walk into the room ready to work.
I pull the light switch.
On the bench a roll's left out
and there's Carmen Miranda
balancing a head full of exotics.
I never saw that before.
Is that a terrapin dancing
in time with a hummingbird
to the sweet music of longevity?

"Basket" was a print block cut by Dorothy Larcher. It was one of the first blocks she cut and one of her most poplar prints.

"Lizard"

'I should love to meet the person who did it.'
Dorothy Larcher to Eve Simmonds

Coming into the room with Eve,
ever so quick, at first I didn't alight
upon the vigour of bite after bite,
of twisted white, that basked
over a rock of indigo.

How could I with embroideries
ringed, strewn around?
Some lay face down,
others flip-sided
on a sagging chair, arm of a sofa;
& I had to stop myself thinking –
as most embroiderers do –
that I prefer the wizardry
of the back to the front.

& it wasn't long before we settled,
as evening light
did amongst a play of bearded irises.
A moment kidnapped. An Indian dusk,
that in this country I'd not thought possible.
A garden in heat, strapped with canna lilies
growing six feet in six seconds rather than a season.

a breeze off a yellowing broom brushes me back,
 I can see the crook of the old one printing,
India shot, rattling around a wrist
as she strikes & releases, strikes & releases,
sraring white hot, white hot, scattering lizards
from beneath a rock, as purple shadows

creep along the selvedge.

Indian shot are the seeds of the Canna lily, when dried they are used as beads for jewellery. Eve Simmonds was an embroiderer and friend of Dorothy Larcher. This was the first time that Dorothy Larcher had ever encountered the work of Phyllis Barron. The print was called Lizard and was printed from an old French block.

Morris Saw A Persian Carpet

I'm thinking of Auden & MacNeice,
their trip to Iceland seeing
only *Stones, More Stones & All Stones*,
Nothing but the bare floorboards
of 1930's, Europe; countries bleached
& stripped,'patched & spliced,
borders driven within an inch,
borders jabbed & segmented,
unpinned overridden, knocked back
inside the grain of life.

I'm thinking of Morris, his trip to Iceland,
how he saw things different,
not seeing *Stones, More Stones & All Stones*,
but a Persian carpet as he wandered,
pondered, prising secrets from the ears
of purple cranesbills, composing Arcadian music.
Morris who cooked over a campfire
a ring saga of plovers, who noticed
like a cloth finisher notices
not *Stones, More Stones & All Stones,*
but threads, grid marks, pink tufts
& Janey's grape-vine hair in swathes,
a sudden blood rush blush of bladder campion.

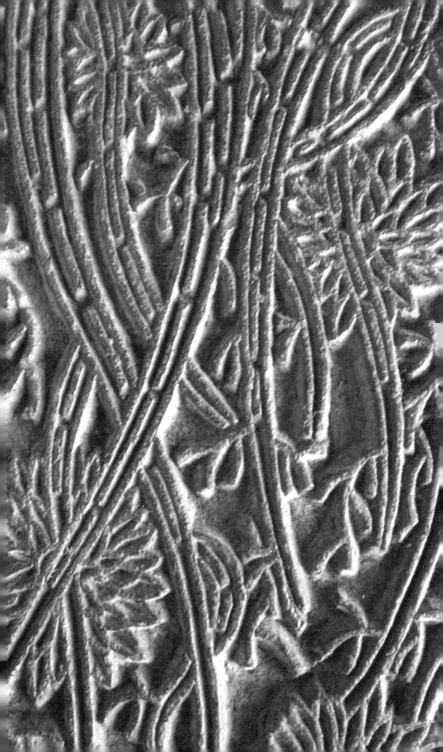

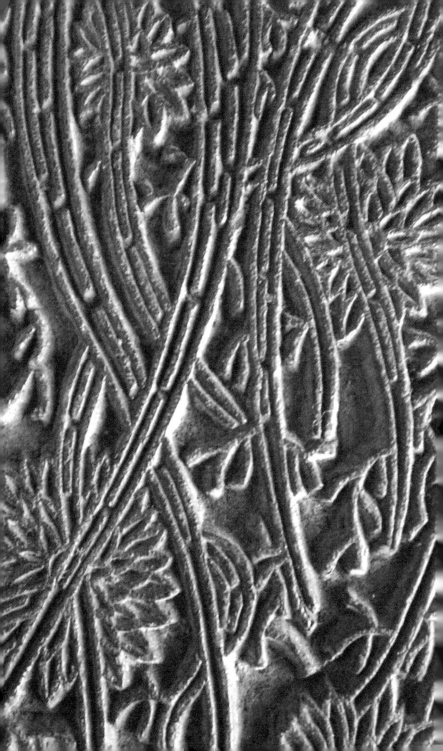

Printed Stuffs

Walking The Blocks, Blocks, Blocks

"Mairet"
(mallet strike)
 Indigo Discharge on Cotton

"Winchester"
(mallet strike)
Indigo Printed on Heavy Natural Linen

"Girton"
(mallet strike)
Indigo Discharge on Linen

"Christmas"
(mallet strike)
On Fine Natural Linen

"Octopus"
(*mallet strike*)
Composed of three blocks,
printed in Grey,
Red and Black

"Clifford"
(mallet strike)
Red Alizarin on Fine Natural Silk

"Basket"
(mallet *strike*)
Unbleached Linen with a Positive Black Print

"Portarlington"
mallet strike)
In Brown on Crepe- de- Chine

"French Dot"
(mallet strike)
Natural Holland, Steeped in Powdered Oak Galls

Swatch

I stand in front of the bedroom window
holding a vase of lichen-sponged twigs.
Wands of sulphur yellow, of turmeric yellow
blobs of sage green, mattress ticking black-blue,
the sort of stuff they charge an arm & a leg at Liberty.
Stuff, just lying around, stuff collected
from the floor up at Pic Tor,
strewn amongst the standing stones at Stanton Moor.

I bought an overcoat today, the sort that stands
off a coat hanger, not hangs off a coat hanger.
The tweed's Scottish, a Galloway, a brutal thirties
herringbone, big thick herringbones,
the sort you choke on, herringbones,
peaty, bracken rotting browns,
chicken liver, pinkie browns, duck-beak-flecked.

Handloom woven, tough enough to kip
in a starry bog all night.
Crumpled, stiff, set with frost,
moulded somehow to the tuneless, lonesome dosser,
& hand sewn button holes, that my boy James
would have made had he been a tailor: then.

Old, older than its wartime issue cut-cake symbol.
It'd do the lads in Belfast, a dealer in the Titanic Quarter
told me as I showed it him.
They like big overcoats, wrap around the body overcoats,
wrap not once but twice overcoats,
overcoats that tie, button to the top.
That overcoat there would do a lot of lads
who drink in Botanic,
a hip flask would slip easy inside the inside pocket.

I thought Phyllis would have worn the coat with her brogues,
                                        inside the workshop.
I thought I bought it for the tweed, the flecks, its Scottish
                Ulsterness, its porridgeness, Demerara sugarness,
reminding me of Dorothy's palette;
spice trade, beneath the arms, where the wear was,
withered vanilla pods & kedgeree & Kipling;
she turned her back on all of them.

Coat, empty of man, I watch it hang on the peg,
partake of its own jauntiness.

Overprinting

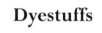

Dyestuffs

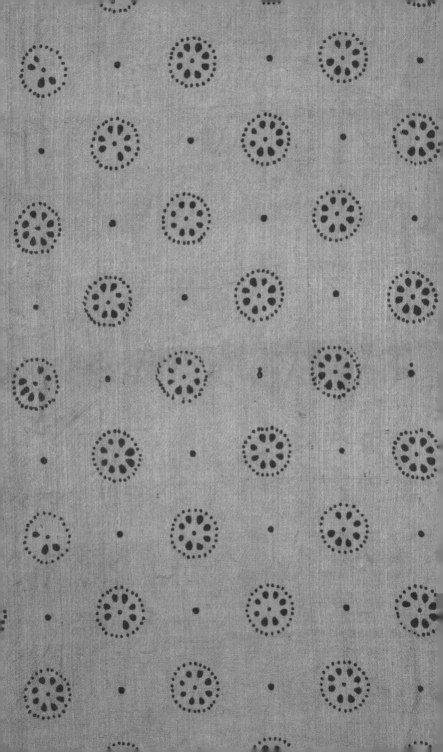

Plants That Dye Yellow, Yellow, Yellow

Agrimony, *Agrimonia eupatoria.*
(Mordant, wash & rinse)

Bog Myrtle or Sweet Gale, *Myrica gale.*
(Mordant, wash & rinse)

Broom, *Sarothammus scoparius.*
(Mordant, wash & rinse)

Crab-Apple, *Pyrus malus.* Fresh inner bark.
(Mordant, wash & rinse)

Gorse, *Ulex europoeus*, Bark, flowers & young shoots.
(Mordant, wash & rinse)

Bramble, *Rubus fructicosus.*
(Mordant, wash & rinse)

Ash, *Fraxinus excelsior*, Fresh inner bark.
(Mordant, wash & rinse)

Common Dock, *Rumex obtusifolius*, Root.
(Mordant, wash & rinse)

Barberry, *Berberis vulgaris,* Stem & Root.
(Mordant, wash & rinse)

Bracken, *Pteris aquiline*, Roots also young tops.
(Mordant, wash & rinse)

Dyer's Greenwood, *Genista tinctoria*, Young Shoots & Leaves.
(Mordant, wash & rinse)

Bog Ashphodel, *Narthecium ossifragum*
(Mordant, wash & rinse)

Hornbeam, *Carpinus betulus,* Bark.
(Mordant, wash & rinse)

Overprinting, Resuscitating, No! Nothing is Dead…

I hold a paperweight in my hand, though I'm not sure if this is what it's called. At any rate it's heavy, solid enough to hold a wedge of paper down; it's a novelty item I've had since I was a child. I haven't shaken it for years.

I shake it, the ground erupts, snowflakes whirl, drive hard against the bubble of plastic; now I know how Lockwood felt on his way to see his landlord, the infant-like sense of anticipation and trepidation.

But the landscape here is gentler, the hills undulate, ahead a lane winds and twists as if dolly-mangled, and a car, just visible, slow and steady, nudges through the giddiness of the snowstorm. Inside the car are two women, Phyllis Barron and Dorothy Larcher, partners in block printing. The car sways in the white squall; it's treacherous driving without chains, and as the flakes settle then ease off, snow covers banks and hedgerows where soon hound-yellow primroses will stipple and nests will be made and fill with life when it melts.

Both women are in their forties, it's the 19th March 1930; Phyllis Barron's birthday, a momentous day for the two women, for today they are moving out of London to a large Georgian house with a walled garden and a stable block for workshops. Hambutts House is situated in Edge Road, a quiet lane, leading off the main street in Painswick, Gloucestershire and Phyllis and Dorothy have worked towards this home and out-house block of soon-to-be converted workshops, an idyll they've dreamed of, will pattern together, a home as a hive of creating and making with all its comings and goings. Their business card announces the change of address and invites visits; there's a sense of rapture and anticipation, now they have left Hampstead, for space and the country, to live and make their 'Hand-Block-Printed Stuffs'. A card declares their intention, announces their varied talents and ambitions.

' Furnishing and dress- stuffs can be chosen here under very pleasant conditions. Patterns and lengths of stuff can be posted to you on your approval. Please say whether you wish to see silk, velvet, or cotton for dresses, or linen and cotton for furnishings.We have light coats of printed handwoven cotton, linen, silk and velveteen which are very useful in the summertime and will wash or clean well'.

As they turn into the driveway they look down the lane, London is nowhere to be seen, covered in snow, and it's picking up again as I tilt the plastic bubble. London is there, but for the moment it's covered, and when the snow melts London will reappear, though it will look different, viewed from a distance, from what it was at the start.

Rummage for an early block print by Phyllis Barron, the piece that Dorothy found at Eve Simmond's house, known as 'Lizard', and wait on the two women, their first meeting at Brook Street Gallery, wondering what the merge will do to their designs. Only now can we understand how the 'early Barron' achieved black by printing with pyrolignite of iron on grey linen prison sheeting from the Caledonian market, or wartime balloon cotton steeped with powdered oak galls, or understand the hours she spent cutting 'Log' trying to get the pattern to repeat through the natural grain.

Going over it again, time after time, it all becomes complex. There's the Russian Block bought at Madame Pagowskis' shop or one of the French Blocks, from Normandy, brought back when Phyllis Barron was only fifteen. And what of her first partner, Frances Woollard; we know little of her except that she too was a block printer, there was a fall-out and Dorothy moved in. The pace of their lives becomes more frenetic as the workloads increase, the tempo is upped, the rhythms and patterns, the iambic of their printed stuffs is breaking and Phyllis is 'thirsting for colours'.

Pick through the London origins, through their champions: Detmar Blow, Muriel Rose, Ethel Mairet, and the numerous exhibiting little galleries, The Major Gallery, The Three Shields Gallery, The Red Rose Gallery, The New Hand Workers Gallery, The Little Gallery. Muriel Rose helped, placed and positioned Phyllis and Dorothy's printed stuffs in context by exhibiting the 'new' printed stuffs with private textile collections, a guide from which Phyllis and Dorothy emerged. Glance from side to side, waft up and down, lift the edges, peer behind, and contemplate the future.

Overprint, the field hospital and Belgium, Ajanta Caves and India, separate and together, Frances and Christiana, London and Gloucestershire, I shake the bubble, again the blizzard swirls. Where does pattern begin or end or does it end, does it carry on, overlap, double back, loop, swagger, tie up tight or swerve?

Overprint, and so a length of stuff is dyed, re-dyed, smoothed out for printing. A block is cut, the dye pad loaded and the mallet struck as the block walks backwards and forwards across the cloth. A length is done, inspected, does the imagined pattern work, is nothing lost or everything gained?

Overprint. Remember 'Motor' embellished with a pastry cutter, rubber nailbrush for spotting. Or 'Jasmine', a version of 'Jasmine', printed in black, overprinted with an unnamed block, printed in yellow on white cotton, or 'Thrush Over Todd', 'Todd' on natural linen, overprinted with 'Thrush'. And sometimes a block is not found, a block won't do.

Overprint, a seed head, mollusc shell, pastry wheel, pastry cutter, nibs and brush heads, all marshalled for spotting, flicking and dabbing, as in 'Chanel' and its unorthodox dab of indigo.

And there, Phyllis in the converted stable block, in overalls, stooped over, saying to Dorothy, "No, nothing is dead", and just like a conversation, the pattern is settled and repeated, comes ricocheting, and every time the pattern's different or at least a variation, and sometimes letting the pattern lie a while before the pattern wakes and leaps and bounds, alive again, is more true still, or so it seems in the retelling, for nothing goes to waste, nothing is dead.

Phyllis and Dorothy vanish beneath the snow but they can be traced and retraced. As the snow settles and the last doiled flake finds its place amid the puzzle of whiteness overprinting, there they are walking from the car, Phyllis almost through the door, Dorothy with a basket close behind. I shake the bubble, and the pattern whirls.

Dorothy to Phyllis

Influence

In the early years
drawing in art class,
turning a lustre jug
filled with the firstlings
of spring,
giving myself
strictly no more than
thirty seconds each side,
how little did I know
I'd soon repeat this task,
amid forms that take
in the whole of you.
Phyllis, your eyes are gimlets
intent, field walking
our quercitron print;
& I feel how it is,
the scuffing, slubs & flaws.
How your heart flounders,
helpless under my influence.

You Let Me In

on your bold geometrics
comprised of large set-in-your-ways
wide harlequins, diamonds, chevrons,
stripes, battleship zigzags,
small spots, pips, rings.

I let you in
on my relaxed pictorial,
comprised of set-in-my-ways
garlands, baskets, ribbons, bouquets,
tied tight with twine, tied twice,
clipped meandering stems.

Inspecting our lengths
we see how larking lines,
irregular graining,
loosens each others blank bits,
how brighter combinations;
such as pure alizarin
when stoked,
bring forth a mightier red,
drive home.

Your Patterns Express So Much

& mine so little, I feel supplanted
by your sense of verticals,
diagonal axes, your use of dumbed-down,
earthy tones, rust, iron mould & indigo.

For years I couldn't shake off
the strangle of Morris's *Acanthus,*
suffocating beneath the leaf shed
of apple, cherry, lemon, vine.

Nothing compared to your spearhead,
flint napped "*Spine*".

For years I couldn't shake off
the smother of Morris's *Strawberry Thief*,
suffocating beneath the mulch
of apple, cherry, lemon, vine.

I was a speck, next to your strong sense
of vertical, diagonal axes.

Old traditions dictate adherence to The Masters.

Mmmmmmmm

Phyllis, just this second I broke through.

Don't Tell Phyllis

I binned an overprint today.

Three times stars shattered to my touch,
three times zigzags blunted,
bashing the selvedge.

Dots went dotty & dashes,
despite my iron grip, slunk off.
In a fit of pique I binned it.

Don't tell Phyllis. Don't!

Why, as I shut the door,
run like pipe-work into the kitchen,
do I feel like a murderess?

Sleeveless

I stand well back from the gravel, stare.
You're posing in a sleeveless, summer, shift dress.
"Little Flower"? Or a print we never named
but should have named *"Catherine Earnshaw's Ghost"*
or simplified to *"Window Pane"* or *"Smash"* or *"Breakthrough"*.

And even though the war mounts us like a rapist,
I manage to make you laugh, darling, with your hair
scraped back, bright tip of your cigarette,
like a Moulin Rouge punter, smouldering,
& your block printer's arms ripe as cantaloupes,
& your block printers wrists turn,
tapering like cabriole legs.

I want to sit you down, I'll kick off my shoes,
go all baby, stroke you with my stockinged legs,
so satiny, so foxglovey, so smoothy, up & down,

up &

White Rabbit Drawn From A Hat

Take the magician & her hat.
Her hand looks right holding a top hat,
it's the right sort of hat, black silk hat,
& she's positioned perfectly.
In her hand she holds a wand & taps,
a puff of purple smoke, perhaps a joke?
Deep down you know it would be wrong
if a rabbit didn't materialise, a rabbit never dies.
By its ears its outline comes out clean.
You can't turn it on or press a button,
stuff happens, a rabbit's drawn from a hat.
It's always a marvel, sense of relief.

Tin Prints

Today a ghost of a man with a hounds tooth cap
brought a bag of empty tins to our door,
saying, *a bite to eat in exchange for these Miss.*
He must have trudged for miles.
As he spoke steam spiralled, séance from his mouth.
I didn't turn him away, as some would, nor did I do
as Dorothy Wordsworth did, couched in cold comfort
offer him a rind of stale bread or drain & drain again
more dregs from a mash, four times already mashed
of black, bitter, tea. I couldn't put him out the back.

I signalled *sit down*, he'd heard we mixed
stuff, possessed the knack to fix, to draw *stuff out of things,*
had possession of the block & things,
printed not what we saw but what we felt & more,
had a fondness for hedgerows,
of women that *Go tell the cat*, those that *wasted nowt.*
Miss a bite to eat in exchange.
Tins tumbled on the rush-mat floor, tins galore,
I washed and stacked, peeled blistered labels,
built a Henge across the drainer,
some like Alpine cowbells dinted
I beat back to shape.

Tin at a time I painted, sponged bands of edelweiss,
lion's paw, in tribute to the mountains' awe,
in tribute to the romantics, dabbed
rock footprints of surefooted ibex, salamander, chamois,
capercaille, sponged like a brow, scores of rock jasmine.

I think he stopped & watched, but I was so immersed!

Phyllis & Dorothy

Duet, Thinking Back Through "Lizard", Thinking Back Through "Basket"

(to the sounds of walking blocks)

(Phyllis to Dorothy)

I've heard folk say "Lizard's"
an early Barron, incomplete without you.

(Dorothy to Phyllis)

I've heard folk say "Basket's"
an early Larcher, incomplete without you.

(Phyllis and Dorothy)

We've heard folk say our "Little Feather"
flew, flew, flew..

"Portarlington"
(Phyllis to Dorothy)

"Portarlington"? Hold on, let me think, I'm looking.

The ledger shows a tiny sample for a scarf,
scrappy, but it's crepe-de-chine!

Gorgeous! Fabulous! Phenomenal!

Here we have another piece.
Neck scarf, block printed in unblinded silk,
galled & bordered with "Eve", dye's muriate of iron.

The records show the Lady never paid.
Anglo-Irish, I wrote, tried to persuade.
So long ago I've forgotten how much we made.

(Dorothy to Phyllis)

"Portarlington", it seems an age.
& the scarf. Yes. It was a scarf, such a timeless thing,
finer than a wedding ring, as slippy.

(Phyllis to Dorothy)

I know I shouldn't but I have this image,
of wig powder drifting from her peak,
sipping tea from the white fright of Belleek.
It's weird how silence makes the image grow.

(Dorothy to Phyllis)

I'd have another go, do write again.

(Phyllis to Dorothy)

They shoot donkeys don't they?

Rehearsing "Portarlington"

Dorothy, it won't be necessary to reveal "Portarlington",
though if needs must, one may hold the spell book up,
flutter the page, as if it were a moth in an opium filled room;
for it's the sounds of the words they've come for,
& like thick fog they'll soon settle down.

I'll sit on a bamboo blossoming chair. You stand in the fray
green shadows of chenille. Darling, do wear your mauve,
with the moons. Fix to your throat the Ruskin brooch
I brought for you, the one that makes you look
like Lady Bracknell or a music hall Everard.
From this distance the stone looks as if it would turn stiffly,
but turn nonetheless, like valves embedded
in the heels of Jason's Towering Talos, I've often wondered
if I came this close & turned would you spill & weaken?

Phyllis, all over the house the audience gathers, cushioned
& propped. It's time. Cover with scarves of pansy printed silk
the parrot cage. Like Mrs Sappho's salon of the 1890's,

No Men

*

We begin, sail close to the edge of pattern. New Worlds.

Pauses, pauses are where one gets off and the other steps in.
Then the ending comes, too brutally soon,
like the snuff of a candle or Diaghilev jolt.
Be sure of this, afterwards a hermaphrodite
will call a moments silence
& we will catch our breath before the whiskey tea's upon us.

Retrospective
(Dorothy to Phyllis)

This fashion, this curator's trendy fashion
for laying flat, like frozen Lakes,
lengths of our printed stuffs is ignorant, flawed, duff.

Exhibit One, Laid Flat:
"Dent" – Printed in Red on Heavy Undyed Linen.

(Phyllis to Dorothy)

Yes. Can't guess what's got into them.
Why flat? Why not draped?
Like the Lincoln Imp, bane of Medieval craftsmen,
flitting from gargoyle to glass, mischief making.

Exhibit Two, Laid Flat:
"Octopus" – Composed of three blocks
printed in Grey, Red & Black

(Dorothy to Phyllis)

Take a page from the trade,
don't they know how lengths display?

Exhibit Three, Laid Flat:
"Mairet", Indigo Discharge on Cotton.

(Phyllis to Dorothy)

Yes. Prints furl, ridges around prize ram's horns,
Fine cottons, silks, lawns.

Exhibit Four, Laid Flat:
"Leon", Indigo discharge in Heavy Natural Linen

(Dorothy to Phyllis)

Yes. We printed flat, long into the night,
our steady hand to eye vision knowing how it draped.

(Jane)

Yes. The repeats should be in motion,
how Tin Tin runs with Snowy.

Printed Stuffs

Walking the Blocks, Blocks, Blocks

"French Dot"
(mallet strike)
Natural Holland, Steeped in Powdered Oak Galls

"Elizabethan"
(mallet strike)
White Balloon Cotton with and Indigo Print

"Clifford"
(mallet strike)
Red Alizarin on fine Natural Silk

"Basket"
(mallet strike)
Unbleached Linen with a positive Black Print

"Octopus"
(mallet strike)
Composed of three blocks, printed in Grey, Red and Black

"Scallop"
(mallet strike)
Galled Linen in Iron

"Spine"
(mallet strike)
Printed in Blue on Undyed Organdie

"Winchester"
(mallet strike)
Indigo Printed on Heavy Natural Linen

"Girton"
(mallet strike)
Indigo Discharge on Linen

"Jasmine"
(mallet strike)
printed in red on balloon cotton
printed in blue on Fine Silk
printed in black on crepe silk over bands of red dots
printed in black over an unnamed block printed in yellow in
white cotton.

Fathoming the Repeat

Dyestuffs

Plants Which Dye Purple, Purple, Purple

Sundew, *Drosera*
(Mordant, wash & rinse)

Damson, Fruit.
(Mordant, wash & rinse)

Bryony, *Bryonia dioice*. Berries
(Mordant, wash & rinse)

Dandelion, *Taraxacum dens-leois*. Roots
(Mordant, wash & rinse)

Whortleberry or Blaeberry, *Vaccinium myrtillus*.
(To Dye wool & silk without mordant,, wash and rinse)

Danewort, *Sambucus ebulus*. Berries
(Mordant, wash & rinse)

Deadly nightshade, *Atropa belladonna*.
(Mordant, wash & rinse)

Elder, *Sambucus nigra*. Berries
(Mordant, wash & rinse)

All Passions Become Strength

I stand outside her door. It's plain, balanced, understated; if it were a person, perfectly dressed. It does not scare me, it has no doorknocker that speaks directly to me like Ebenezer Scrooge's doorknocker, nothing spirals from its mouth, snow does not fall, bells are silent. I remember the first time I came to her door, I was in tears and I'm glad now that she wasn't in, for the person she would have seen was not an accurate portrayal of the person I've become.

Our time together proved formative, our time apart more so. I was studying the New Zealand short story writer Katherine Mansfield and I remember being struck by the first question she asked me, 'Are you in love with her?'

Instinctively I knew she already knew the answer; I was. This she told me confidently was my problem. I had to get rid of Katherine, I remember thinking which one. I had to fall out of love with the marmoset, the 'civet cat' as Virginia Woolf called her, I had to get shot if I was going to write anything coherent. This, she said, is when I'll gain ground and ultimately strength.

Turning on her chair, and I see her now laughing, she walked with me like Aristotle through the dapple of a glade, guided me through the phases. In retrospect I recognise, firstly, and not uniquely, the struck by a lightning bolt moment, then something close to terminal, when research becomes nothing more than breaking the spines of books, more books and only books. And eventually, like summer light taunting a drawn curtain there's the dawn of identification, the 'she speaks directly to me and only me' phase, followed by the stalking, riffling through drawers, portmanteaus, wardrobes, the frequent sightings on the bridge, across the street, then embarrassingly, she came to me at night.

She raised her eyebrows when I told her I thought I was getting consumption saying, 'its just a cold, you'll shake it off', and she was right, it WAS just a cold! Though not once did she ever mock passion, fantasy and delusion; yes, but never passion, for if the passion gets lost amongst the cynicism and reductionism or a person's pure conceit, then there never will be any true writing. The fire is the best place for that.

The desire to be near to, or go to the places the person or persons had once been is natural. In this case, there was Edith Simcox; she told me about the place in Soho, a philanthropist's Shirt Making Factory, a womens' co-operative, set up by Simcox and her co- partner Mary Hamilton. Hamilton & Co began life at 68 Dean Street, Soho, London, moving to Mortimer Street, Cavendish Square. She spoke of how she was so taken by Edith's words, her driving passion, addressed in her article 'Eight Years of Co-Operative Shirt making' in which she states her commitment to 'a Co-Operative Workshop, where the shirt makers should be their own employers, and divide amongst themselves the whole price paid by the hosier to the contractor'. She described her sneaky peek up the stairs, as a student, whilst the workshop was being restored. The endless hydra-like sewing machines left abandoned, needles poised, mid-needle, only just this minute left, discarded aprons along a bench, fine cotton filaments and fibres feathering the air that bring to mind the line in Mrs Gaskell's *North and South*, 'I have seen hell and it is white'. But this is nowhere near as bad as the mill, this was

the imagination mining, where fantasy and reality intersect.
She understood when I spoke, melodramatically, of needing to
witness the flowering of an Aloe.

So how do we define Phyllis and Dorothy against the age,
against their peers and other practitioners, against each
other? Do I make them into my puppets, active with a
series of imaginary threads? When people ask me were they
'together' or when people ask me to 'put them together' with
a diagnostic tool, for the sake of framing, recovery or for the
sake of others, it's difficult; I don't know what to say, or have
the right to say. Some say they were devoted; in Painswick I
was told they were known as the 'Barrons'.

I can only go back to their 'printed stuffs'. Dorothy and Phyllis
for the moment must step back from the curtains, step into
the corridor, walk around the physic garden, trample across
the calamine lawn, whilst I take you to one of their important
commissions, 'Girton Curtains ', and say that their English
eclecticism, their subversive dialogues inspired by numerous
design sources, in pattern design and interior decoration
culminated in harmony, balance and unity within the whole
ambience of their rooms,

Of course, you were right,
about the need for neutral blinds –
dark string –
to prevent fading .

What was it you said?
must not colour the light in the room,
not in any way.

Together they challenged the notions of the established

academic order, as did their designs for Girton College
Cambridge, the Combination Room and Fellow's Dining
Room in the early thirties. Records and correspondence show
that a battle over the commission ensued. A more masculine,
Edwardian look was preferred, 'antiques', and 'curtains
of a richer appearance', instead of block printed- semi-
abstract designs, oak tables, parchment lamps, Kelim rugs,
unpainted plaster walls, single flower glasses. It was perhaps
this direct challenge that unnerved the Fellows, the lack of
institutionalised masculinity the room suggested, that asked
questions about their authority and which the Fellows wished
by revamping the rooms, to mimic the studious nature of
the mens' Colleges. It was perhaps this triumph, Phyllis and
Dorothy's passion as hand makers of their work that answers
part of the question. It is true that the inter-war period was
an open window onto an avenue populated with women hand
makers.

The Arts and Crafts movement provided a creative space
and an independent income for middle-class women. Phyllis, we know had a small private allowance, Dorothy less so,
though neither woman was poor or wanting. As Tanya Harrod
observes, 'The crafts operated as a third space between better
defined activities of fine art and design'.

Like many women makers of the time, Phyllis and Dorothy
never married, a number of factors may have contributed;
the lack of men after the war, and the growing confidence
amongst modern crafts women that they would be able to
work without the problematic responsibility of childcare and
running a household. Importantly, networks were established
with other women makers, and we can see this with Dorothy
and Phyllis, and their relationship with the weaver and dyer
Ethel Mairet, the patron and entrepreneur Muriel Rose, Jean

Orage, and wealthy women such as Margaret Pilkington, involved in exhibiting societies, setting up the Red Rose Guild of Artworkers in 1921, and in Dorothy Elmhirst through commissioning work. Muriel Rose, especially championed the printed stuffs of Phyllis and Dorothy.

How Phyllis and Dorothy lived in the house they had yearned for we can only guess. The reportage of colleagues, apprentices and friends like Enid Marx, Robin Tanner, Susan Bosence describe a paradise of rooms and fruitful gardens, but we can never know how they lived inside these rooms, the gardens we can never walk in, or overhear the conversations in a workshop. Dorothy's watercolour paintings offer some perception, connections with her printed designs and there is a marriage of sorts in the forty or so watercolours. There is also the transcript of a talk given by Phyllis, *My Life As A Hand Block Printer*, at Dartington, but very little in comparison to their 'printed stuffs'; their auto/biography on cloth not paper.

Like so many women makers of the period, unmarried, childless, the stereotype of the funny, eccentric aunts who threw pots, spun, wove, block printed, embroidered, most records are lost or forgotten, thought of little worth; not widely honoured or preserved. Even when they are retained, especially personal letters and correspondence are often edited or withheld from public view. The men makers fared better; most had families and most of their archives, as with Bernard Leach and Michael Cardew, are preserved by their wives, children and public institutions. Not so the women makers, childless, unmarried, with many all we have are fragments, the bottom of a cooking pot.

Phyllis and Dorothy were fortunate, befriended by the artist, etcher, and educationalist Robin Tanner and his wife Heather, who persuaded them both of the enormous value of their work and printed stuffs and embarked on a project to create a unique record in two majestic tomes, along with a cornucopia of their personal and business lives. Their archive, left to the Tanners, was preserved with all its wonders, and when Phyllis, who thought what she had achieved with Dorothy was very little, by some chance enters the room where the books are laid out for viewing, when Phyllis, prompted by Dorothy to turn, turn the page, turning page, after page, now together, re-live the patterns, the life, death and near deaths of their prints, delighting upon dyes triumphant fading, the rhythms are still vital, still vigorous with making.

Gathering Home Grown Flowers
From Our Painswick Garden

Stage lit by the sun, I stand
at the southern edge of our flowerbed.
Day lilies crane beside ruddy brick
as flights of dragon flies overprint.
I stoop, cut trails of indigo clematis,
blackcurrant pansies, an array
of Agamemnon old gold
 polyanthus for you to paint.

I look back, Dorothy, is that your shadow by the bay
where the room suddenly darkens,
or your bearded yellow iris shawl
over shoulders falling,
as you walk away. It must be seconds ago
you were there , I'm sure, arranging
in a Leach studio pot something
unheard of to doze.

Today, your name seems permanent,
resistant to what makes bleed or fuzz.
I balance each letter between each taken breath:
with every step I'm stashing colours,
with every stem I pick & loop & thread,
with every every tendril torn, every flower head,
wasp hollowed, bee begged, I'll cling.

Painting Home Grown Flowers
From Our Painswick Garden

I watch you from a downstairs window,
lingering on torcs of cigarette smoke
choking a shabby tea rose, lilac lamb tails of wisteria,
your shoulders rising like a crown,
announcing us across your shift dress
in the bruise print blues of "*Elizabethan*".

Intent, you pick out the school scarf, sun stripes,
wrap them around your neck
& Phyllis, I sense you're worrying,
burrowing like a death watch beetle
inside the rafters of your head,
worrying about what lies ahead,
now war is here again,
though don't we have it all, with more to come?

Stiffening, I overprint as day sinks into night,
then rises into day, & I turn my face away
from your face, face that betrays a shadow.

Is that my shadow by the bay? Slip of a thing
shrivelling by the ruddy brick,
ducking at the sight of dragonflies,
shrugging at the sight of a runaway shawl,
bearded yellow iris shawl,
over shoulders, over my shoulders falling.

I walk toward my easel, thick clots of leached hydrangeas,
black pansies, white centaureas, pheasant eye, violets
vowing not to let pass as green passes through into indigo,
what we achieved, or else as with the craftiness of time,
let all we made be scuppered.

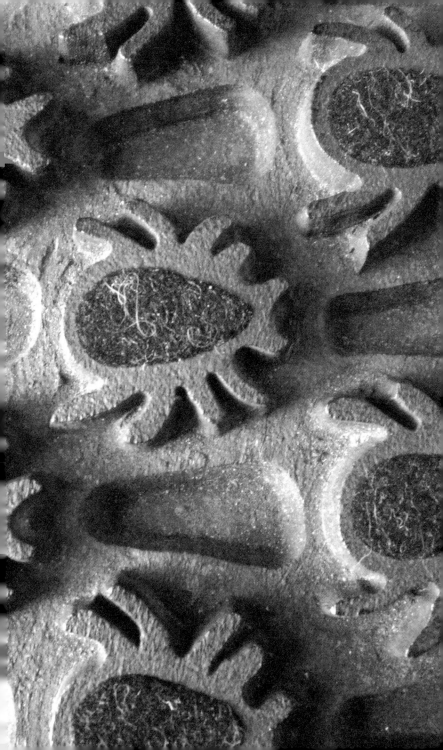

Printed Stuffs

Walking the Blocks, Blocks, Blocks

"Log"
(mallet strike)
Iron on Linen

"Scallop"
(mallet strike)
Galled Linen in Iron

"Dandelion"
(mallet strike)
Printed in Iron on Yellow Silk

"French Dot"
(mallet strike)
natural Holland,
Steeped in Powdered Oak Galls

"Winchester"
(mallet strike)
Indigo printed on heavy Natural linen

"Dent"
(mallet strike)
printed in red on heavy undyed linen

"Spine"
(mallet strike)
printed in blue
on undyed Organdie

"Girton"
(mallet strike)
Indigo discharge on
Linen

"Chanel"
(mallet strike)
only a fragment left.

I Am Phyllis Barron,
I Am Dorothy Larcher

Longhi's Villa; it's late afternoon, outside the unbearable
hillside afa. Inside the shutters folded, still no let up. I have
my back to the door; my glass of Pelagrino is flat, still as a lazy
English millpond. A potted olive flicks on the terrace. A spider
rolls up a fly and puts it to bed. Luca is back, I hear his car
winding its way through the gates, though he won't disturb
me until later. I might go on looking and listening forever. I
might find a box with bright strings of beads, jewels like facts
and more facts I'd missed. I might uncover and shake a bolt of
French Toile, Toile de Jouy in mouse back or ointment pink,
I might trace through the scratch and copper plate the two
of you, Phyllis younger than I imagined wearing a "Gaskell"
dress, Dorothy, stronger than I imagined wearing a "Basket" or
"Lizard" skirt, in a colour I'd not seen, or dreamed of.

If I can find a box big enough, a trunk, I'll climb inside and
close the lid, and if I have one, I'll light a match or flick
the wheel-strike of a lighter; now where shall I go? I wade
through the clothes, for there are clothes and shoes and
hats and various purses and dolly bags, housecoats, aprons,
gowns, strange drawstrings and weird almost anatomical bony
handles that feel like the edge of a shoulder blade, a breast
bone, columns of vertebra that clash and contrast against
pockets of sweet peas, tea rose day silks, the Chinese pagoda
that straddles night printed satins, Fortuny velvets; I'll wade
through all of this for they have risen to the surface like water
lilies. I'll not do as Henry James did, row out into the lagoon
at midnight and drown and drown and drown again dear
Constance's clothes.

I have my back to the door and my head in the trunk, where to next? The light dips, the glass of water marbles as though a paint brush tip is being dipped, swilled of its watercolour, and there is an intervention, a kafuffle in the room, towards the back, behind me. I swivel, books fall from a shelf, a plumped up cushion collapses, my jacket's pulled and swung, a small woman steps forward. *So she was small*, I say to myself, small and fine, delicate as bone china after all, and she is beautifully dressed, her blouse states "Guinea" with black piped around the cuff-edge, plainly announcing, *I am Dorothy Larcher*, then a tall woman steps forward, struck with purpose and intent, fit for purpose, her hand raised as if to signal, as if to stop me like a train, announcing, *I am Phyllis Barron*, and coming forward they sit beside me, bookends on either side, amidst the avalanche of paper, Alpine range of books and prints, photographs, samples, swatches and happenstance.

Together they talked to me of spells and potions and mad, wild fangled schemes, fairy tales, printed notions of diamonds they never printed, roundels and rosettes they wish they hadn't bothered, and luckily nobody knew of, till now at least. Dorothy spoke of garlands and ribbons, reminded Phyllis of *Boteh,* all their experimental squares and spirals, and Phyllis chastised Dorothy for even thinking Chintz.

Trees they both agreed, gave definition to winter. Unanimous when it came to a vote on birds, leaves and flowers, we all agreed, insect combinations mattered. Phyllis championed France, Zigzags, Chevrons and Ogee, suppressed the war as best she could. Dorothy championed India, Paisley and embroidery, turned her face to the side, fearful when Phyllis spoke of the war, returning to England when she'd buttoned up with a lost 17th century panel of an Indian Elephant she thought she'd left on board a liner.

Between them they argued little, save to say Dorothy ventured she could have painted more than forty-two watercolours, and Phyllis raged against the shrunkeness of her Tiger lilies. Animated they spoke to me of loving cups and loving spoons, of oak and basketry and haven't you guessed delved even deeper into indigo. They spoke of the call, of recognition, of chance encounters, a host of print & dye secrets I should never, no never, *swear after me,* repeat. I seal my lips with waxy red. *My heart is singing like a bird*, I turn to say, but they are gone.

There, In An Ercol Bottom Drawer

After Barron and Larcher

I remember all my early prints, all my experiments, my failures,
my amputees, the gouging & scoring, scars & dents.

I printed
Jackie, Ethel, Joan, because how many times do you see women
as a triumvirate, as musketeers.

I printed
all for one and one for all, Jackie, Ethel, Joan.

I printed;
& he knows who he is, Women, Land & Power In Eighteenth
Century England, because I know he hated me reading it in case I
got funny ideas, which I did.

I printed
you're looking very classical today, & those sea pearls remind me
of my Mother, & why are you reading THAT! He knows nothing
about poetry; which was rich coming from him.

I printed
the word indiscretion, opposite of turn the other cheek.

I printed
hard cop, soft cop routine. More people should be aware of this.

I printed
they get pleasure out of the hard cop, soft cop routine.

I printed
Maggie's photo of a stone on a beach in Wicklow. with mountains
& there was a dog barking at a stone, somebody's dog,

not Maggie's dog, though the dog looked as if it belonged to
Maggie, a wire wool fox terrier it was.

I printed, Oh Maggie! I wish I was there with you.

I printed I can't believe a publisher printed a book entitled
Love Letters of Great Men

I printed what James said Keith said whilst deconstructing
Nelson's Battle of Trafalgar tunic,
'James you have an 18th century body'.

I printed
basting sleeves, 80 wasn't it? Hundreds of pairs of waders
across the flannel.

I printed
buttonholes, buttonholes, every stitch the same,
biggest ever Peter Rabbit Eyes.

I printed
the spider, spinning, stockrooms.

I printed
your face when faced with the brilliant Tommy Nutter.

I printed if you could have seen your face.

I printed
because it needs printing, the idea you don't need pockets
in trousers.

I printed
Giovanni Battista Moroni's, *The Tailor* because it's true what you
said, it's you in a previous life.

I printed
the ruby seal, squat inside The Tailor's signet ring,
thinking, *Sexy, very sexy,*
the way he fiddles with it.

I printed
sexy, very sexy the way he fiddles with it.

I printed
don't ask me where I live, don't even think about it.

I printed
my Palladian apartment in Vicenza...
I know, I know I'm inconsistent.

I printed
Roberto Saviano: Read Him.

I printed
Carlo's assertion that 'Venice is the place you take to bed your
girlfriend', he told me I wouldn't dare too. (I dared to.)

I printed
Delitzia! The Epic History of The Italians And Their Food.

I printed
Pasolini, Roberto Mancini, Isabella Rossellini, .

I printed
but I'd rather eat a yellow Zucchini risotto.

Printing
I'll never forget the taste, because I hadn't eaten for days
& the Doctors at *San Bortolo* performed miracles,
not the Madonna.

I printed
the purr & roar of Lampedusa's *Leopard*.

I printed
Lawrence's *Etruscans*, all of Calvino.

I printed &
what more can I say?

Bibliography

Forster, E. M., *A Passage to India* (Penguin Classics, 2005)

Gilman, C. P., *The Yellow Wallpaper* (Dover Thrift Edition, 1998)

Hamilton, C., *William, an Englishman* (Persephone, 1999)

Harrod, T., *The Crafts in Britain in the 20th Century* (Yale University Press, 1999)

Haycock, D. B., *Paul Nash* (Tate Publishing, 2002)

King, B. M., *Silk and Empire* (Manchester: Manchester University Press, 2005)

Largo, M., *Christiana Herringham and The Edwardian Art Scene* (London: Lund Humphries Publishers, 1996)

Macdonald, L., *The Roses of No Man's Land* (London: Penguin, 1993)

Morris, W., Briggs, A. (Ed.), *William Morris: Selected Writings and Designs* (London: Pelican, 1962)

Nash, P., *Outline: an Autobiography* (London: Columbus Books, 1988)

Polkey, P., 'Recuperating the Love/Passions of Edith Simcox', in Polkey, P. (Ed.), *Women's Lives Into Print: The Theory, Practice and Writing of Feminist Auto/Biography,* (London: Macmillan Press Ltd, 1999)

Roscoe, B., 'Phyllis Barron and Dorothy Larcher', in Greensted, M. (Ed.), *The Arts and Crafts Movement in the Cotswolds*, (Stroud: Sutton Publications, 2001)

Weaver, C.R. 'Introduction', in *Enid Marx and her Circle*, (London: Sally Hunter Fine Art, 1992)

PHYLLIS BARRON &
DOROTHY LARCHER
PAINSWICK, GLOS'

Telephone: Painswick 130.

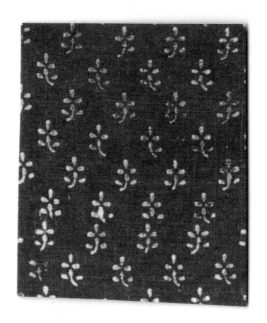

HAND - PRINTED STUFFS
for dresses, fitted upholstery, curtains and covers made to orde
Made coats, bedspreads, shawls, scarves. Parcels can be sent on approv
Visitors to the Cotswolds are invited to see the work in progress and t
finished stuffs, at Painswick. Above is a pattern of our indigo-dyeir